YOU CAN DO IT!
SPELLING

Contents

Meet the
Odd Mob

The Odd Mob is a gang of seven friends – a right rabble of different characters, some cool, some clever and some clots. A quick 'who's who' will tell you what you need to know.

Wozza

Lowdown: questions spin round her head like socks in a tumble dryer.
Likes: question marks
Dislikes: all other punctuation
School report: she loves asking questions – it's a pity she's hopeless at answers.

HMD

Lowdown: this heavy metal dude is the Mob's seriously hairy 70s rocker.
Likes: carrying a guitar at all times, even in the shower.
Dislikes: peace and quiet
School report: a bright pupil whose classic wide-legged stance has greatly improved this year.

Max

Lowdown: Max Mullet is tough, keen and adventurous. Oh, and she's magnetically attracted to trouble.
Likes: having the worst hair in the solar system.
Dislikes: being poked in the eye, liver and fashion.
School report: Maxine is very popular, especially with headlice.

Ulf

Lowdown: half-boy half-beast, Ulf is not only as daft as a brush but looks like one.
Likes: grunting, and doing anything which is a naughty no-no.
Dislikes: soap and ballet
School report: shouldn't he be in the zoo?

YOU CAN DO IT!

SPELLING

Andy Seed and **Roger Hurn**

*Hodder
Children's
Books*

A division of Hachette Children's Books

Text copyright © 2011 Andy Seed and Roger Hurn
Illustrations © 2011 Martin Chatterton
Many thanks to Barbara Seed for acting as consultant on this book

First published in Great Britain in 2011 by Hodder Children's Books

1

ISBN 978 0 340 93120 2

Book design by Fiona Webb
Project editors: Margaret Conroy and Polly Goodman

Printed and bound by CPI Bookmarque Ltd, Croydon, Surrey

The paper and board used in this paperback by Hodder Children's Books
are natural recyclable products made from wood grown in sustainable forests.
The manufacturing processes conform to the environmental regulations
of the country of origin.

Hodder Children's Books
A division of Hachette Children's Books
338 Euston Road, London NW1 3BH
An Hachette UK Company
www.hachette.co.uk

Flash

Lowdown: the fastest girl on the planet, always in a hurry.
Likes: trackies, trainers and treadmills
Dislikes: waiting
School report: English 14%; Maths 9%; Science 11%; PE 253%

Googal

Lowdown: she's so bright her teachers have to wear sunglasses.
Likes: complicated sums
Dislikes: easy listening
School report: if she was any sharper we could use her to cut cheese.

Deej

Lowdown: so cool he makes cucumbers jealous.
Likes: drum 'n' bass
Dislikes: triangles
School report: the brightest thing about him is the bling he wears.

Shagpile

Lowdown: a carpet, with a tail at one end and a cold wet nose at the other.
Likes: bones, bottoms, lamp-posts
Dislikes: cats, postmen, vets
School report: Tail wagging: great; Barking: loud; Biting: useless; Hungry: always

Mr Sumo

Lowdown: a rude wrestler and big bully who is the gang's evil enemy.
Likes: sitting on people
Dislikes: children, old ladies, baby animals and being fair
School report: expelled for eating the photocopier. (Not one of the gang.)

You'll also meet two of the Mob's mates, Cheesy Chad and Multiple Joyce, from time to time – they're fun and full of top tips too.

What's It All About?

A quick quiz:

A) Do you enjoy reading spelling books at school? YES/NO

B) Do you read them when you don't have to? YES/NO

C) Do you only bother with spelling when you have to pass a SATs test? YES/NO

D) Do you think spelling is really boring? YES/NO

If you answered NO for questions A and B and YES to questions C and D then CONGRATULATIONS, you're a normal kid!

And you're smart. You learned how to speak English. And did you need a teacher to help you figure out how to do it? No, you didn't. You learned it when you were a baby – which is pretty amazing. OK. You're great at learning stuff so why do you need this book? Here's the answer. You're already smart but this book can make you smarter at spelling. It's like having an extra brain you can keep in your pocket – only not so squelchy. And you don't have to go to school to read it either.

Questions you won't find answers to in this book

Do steamrollers roll steam?

If you had everything, where would you put it?

Why is the word dictionary in the dictionary?

So what IS in this book?

Help to avoid embarrassing situations like this:

Teacher: *Make a sentence starting with the letter 'I'.*

Pupil: *I is ...*

Teacher: *No, no, no, don't say "I is", you say "I am".*

Pupil: *OK, I am the ninth letter of the alphabet.*

So, as Cheesy Chad says ...

If you want to find out more about spelling – read this book.

If you want to meet the Odd Mob – read this book.

If you want to impress your friends with a load of jokes – read this book.

If you're shipwrecked on a desert island and are starving hungry – eat this book.

If you also need help with punctuation and grammar, there are two more Odd Mob books to sort you out. Remember. You Can Do It!

How the pages work

Story title

Topic

Explanation or examples

Introduction

Illustration showing some examples

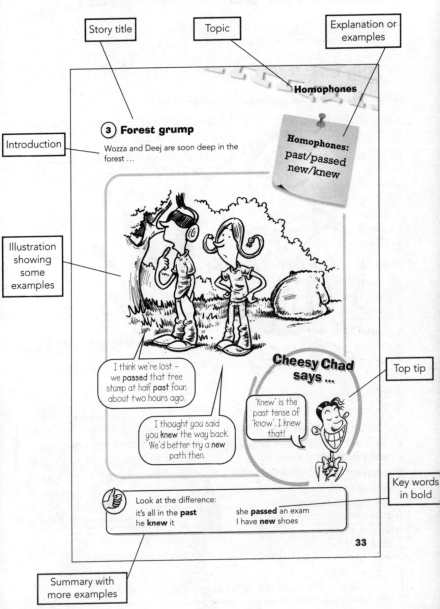

Top tip

Key words in bold

Summary with more examples

Root Words
Putting Down Roots

Root words:
Stand alone

1 Dig this

Ulf is digging up the garden.

Ulf is planting letters of the alphabet because he's hoping they'll grow into **root words**. He'll have a long wait because **root words** don't grow underground – they're words that other words grow out of.

Cheesy Chad says ...

You can use a root word to help you with other spellings.

A **root word** is a word that has nothing added at the beginning or the end. It contains the basic meaning of the word:

Dig is the **root word** for **dig**s, **dig**ger and **dig**ging.

② All in the family

Mr Sumo overdoes it with the cream doughnuts.

Ugly, uglier, ugliest is a word family.

Really? It sounds more like Mr Sumo's family.

Root words:
Belong to word families

Word families grow out of root words.
For example, Mr Sumo is **happy** eating one cream doughnut, **happier** eating five cream doughnuts and **happiest** eating ten cream doughnuts. But he is very **unhappy** when all those cream doughnuts give him a tummy ache.

Joke Break

Q. What's in the middle of nowhere?

A. The letter 'h'.

Can you see how the words **happier**, **happiest** and **unhappy** have all grown out of the root word **happy** to make a **word family**?

If you know the meaning of the root word, you can work out what the words in the **word family** mean.

In a **word family**, all the words share the same root spelling and have a similar meaning, e.g.:

excite   **excit**ed   **excit**able   **excit**ing

③ Growing from the root

The Odd Mob have a competition.

Root words: Grow new words

Quick: quicker, quickly, quickening

Heavy: heavily, heavier, heaviest

Question: questions, questioned, questioning

Cool: cools, uncool, coolly, cooler, coolest

Hair: hairy, hairier, hairiest

Clever: cleverly, cleverer, cleverest

Root: lots of roots

The Odd Mob are trying to see how many words they can grow from a root word – but Ulf doesn't quite get it.

 You can **grow** new **words** from a root word:

hope ▶ hopeful   sad ▶ sadness   enjoy ▶ enjoyment

(4) **Hunt the root**

The Odd Mob are playing a word game.

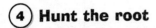

Root words:
More root
words

No, Shagpile, we said we're playing 'Hunt the Root' not 'Hunt the Boot'.

Oi! Give me my shoe back!

The aim of the game is to hunt out the **root words** and underline them. Let's take a peek at how well Googal's doing. She's found them all. But we can't look at Ulf's word sheet – he's eaten it. He says he likes chewing roots!

Hunt the Root

<u>E</u>lectricity

<u>C</u>arefully

<u>D</u>arkness

<u>R</u>eacting

<u>H</u>armful

Here are some more root words that are part of other words:

fearing   **understand**able   un**done**   **use**ful

11

YOU CAN DO IT!

⑤ Double Dutch

Googal's really into root words.

Did you know that lots of English words have their roots in the ancient Latin and Greek languages?

Root words: Some come from Greek and Latin

Yeah, well it's all Greek to me.

Googal's right! At least half of the words in the English language come from Greek and Latin roots. Knowing these roots helps you to understand the meaning of words before you look them up in the dictionary.

Googal's made a study of root words. Take a look at her chart and see which language the words came from.

Multiple Joyce

Which of these is a root?

A liquorice root
B root beer
C rooting tooting
D bus route

English words	Root	Meaning	Language
graph, paragraph	graph	to write	Greek
telephone, phonics	phon	sound	Greek
video, videotape	vid	to see	Latin
vacant, vacuum, evacuate	vac	empty	Latin

Prefixes

Googal results

① **Cop that!**

Sometimes, root words have groups of letters added to them at the beginning to change their meanings.

Max **packed** her bag to go on holiday.
Ulf **unpacked** it.

The letters '**un**' change the meaning of the word.

'**un**' is a **prefix**.

Here are some more prefixes:

Prefix	+	word	=	new word
re	+	move	=	remove
mis	+	take	=	mistake
bi	+	cycle	=	bicycle

Some **prefixes** are words themselves:
underground   **out**side   **over**cook   **up**set

② Know what I mean

Goggal is an expert on prefixes, of course. She knows the meaning of all of them, which helps her to spell well.

Prefixes: Have a meaning

Sub means 'under'. A subway goes under a road.

Is that why I don't understand subtraction?

Anti means 'against'. Anticlockwise means moving against the direction of a clock's hands.

My auntie is against my haircut.

I think my mobile was preshrunk!

Pre means 'before'. With a prepay mobile phone you pay for calls before you make them.

AuntieSocial

Every **prefix** has a meaning:

mis means wrong (misspell)   **semi** means half (semicircle)

trans means across (transfer)   **micro** means small (microscopic)

③ Not much

Googal teaches the gang all about prefixes, including six prefixes that mean 'not'.

Prefixes:
'un', 'dis', 'im', 'in', 'il' and 'ir' mean 'not'

un	HMD's shoes were **un**cool.
dis	Wozza's desk was **dis**organised.
im	Shagpile found food **im**possible to resist.

in	Mr Sumo liked his **in**visible car.
il	Ulf's new pet was **il**legal.

Cheesy Chad says ...

'Un' and 'dis' are the most common of these prefixes.

ir	Flash's trainers were **ir**reparable.

More examples of 'not' **prefixes**:
undo   **dis**obey   **im**patient   **in**valid   **il**logical   **ir**reversible

YOU CAN DO IT!

④ Number won

The gang have entered the local church raffle. They win some interesting prizes.

Max won a **uni**cycle. It has **one** wheel.

Googal won some **bi**noculars. They're for **two** eyes.

Flash won a **tri**pod. It has **three** legs.

Ulf got a small **quad** bike. It has **four** wheels.

Deej won a rubber **cent**ipede. It has **100** legs.

HMD won 500 **milli**litres of treacle. There are **1000** millilitres in a litre.

Wozza got a glass **poly**gon with **many** sides. Mmm, nice …

Joke Break

Q: How do squid get to school?

A: By octobus!

Some **prefixes** stand for **numbers**:

uni – one	**bi** – two	**tri** – three	**quad** – four
pent – five	**cent** – 100	**milli** – 1000	**poly** – many

16

5 Eenie meanie

Once they had wrecked their prizes, Googal told the gang some more prefix meanings.

Prefixes: Learn the meanings

Auto means 'self', like in **auto**graph.

I'm getting someone else to write my **auto**biography.

Fore means 'before', like in **fore**tell.

Anybody heard yesterday's weather **fore**cast?

Inter means 'between', like in **inter**national.

I'm **inter**viewing myself later.

Post means 'after', like in **post**-war.

I always get up after the postman!

More **prefix** meanings:

tele (far off): telescope   **ex** (out of): export

photo (light): photograph

YOU CAN DO IT!

⑥ Naughty naughty

Finally, Googal loses her patience as it becomes clear that the gang are just not listening to her.

Prefixes: Root words stay the same

You should all be less **immature**! It was quite **unnecessary** for you to be so silly. Now you've made me **overreact**!

im + mature = immature
un + necessary = unnecessary
over + react = overreact

Look, the spelling of the root word stays the same when the prefix is added. No letters are taken away or added.

Multiple Joyce

Which of these words has a prefix?

A missile
B miserable
C miscalculation
D Miss World

Hey, they're learning! That will cheer Googal up.

18

Suffixes

Suffix The Matter With the Odd Mob

Suffixes:
End words

1 Hunting for suffixes

Ulf goes hunting.

Ulf is hunting for **suffixes**. He's heard that they end words and he thinks that's a bad thing. So he's trying to catch them before they can end any more.

Googal has to explain to him that **suffixes** aren't word killers, but letters that can be added to the end of words to make new words. Googal says suffixes aren't harmful, but they can sometimes **change** the way the new word they make is **spelled**.

Cheesy Chad says ...

Here are some well known suffixes: 'ed', 'ion', 'ing', 'ful', 'ness', 'er', 'ous'

A suffix is a **word ending** and adding it to a word can **change** the **spelling**:

ease + y = easy   happy + ness = happiness

② He's a headbanger

Ulf's has banged his head playing head tennis with a rock and is seeing **double**.

> I'm seeing double.

> Well you're lucky it's me you're seeing two of and not Mr Sumo.

Suffixes: Words ending with one consonant

Don't worry, Ulf will soon be fine again. And you'll be fine if you remember that normally, when you add a suffix to a word that ends with one consonant, you **double the final letter**. For example, big + er = bi**gg**er.

Cheesy Chad says ...

> A consonant is any letter of the alphabet except a, e, i, o, or u.

 Usually, if a short word ends in a single consonant you **double** the last letter when you add a suffix:

sit + ing = si**tt**ing   run + er = ru**nn**er

3) Double or no double

The gang are playing a spelling game.

**Suffixes:
More than one
consonant**

I've got a rotten voice.

I don't know the words.

SING

Can't I just play guitar?

You're having a spelling test tomorrow, come rain or shine.

The gang are playing a spelling game about adding suffixes. It's called 'Double Letter or Not?' Googal is winning easily. She knows that when a word ends with two consonants or more, you **don't double** the final letter.

So let's hope it snows.

If a word ends with more than one consonant, **don't double** the last letter when you add a suffix:

sing + ing = singing ✓   sing + ing = singging ✗

gru**nt** + ed = grunted ✓   grunt + ed = gruntted ✗

YOU CAN DO IT!

(4) No Show

The Odd Mob go to a concert but they're in for a disappointment.

If a word **ends in 'l'** and you want to add a suffix to it, remember to double the 'l' when you spell the word (eg marvel + ous = marvellous).

The Odd Mob's journey hasn't ended in 'l' but it has ended in disappointment. They've travelled miles to see a gig by Tone Deff, their favourite DJ, only to find that the show's been cancelled.

Usually, if a long word ends with the letter 'l', you **double the 'l'** when adding the suffix:

level + ing = levelling   shovel + ed = shovelled

⑤ **Open wide**

Deej goes to the dentist.

When 'full' is written as a suffix it is always spelled '**ful**' – with only one 'l'. Deej is worried that his visit to the dentist will be full of pain – for the dentist! As it happens, Deej's time in the dentist's chair is delight**ful** even though the dentist refuses to give him chocolate fillings. After all, too much sugar is harm**ful** for your teeth.

The suffix '**ful**' is **always** spelled with **one 'l'**:
beauti**ful**   hope**ful**   spite**ful**   play**ful**

YOU CAN DO IT!

⑥ Googal rapping

Googal can do everything – even rap.

Suffixes:
'y' to 'i' rule

Deej wants to be good at spelling but he doesn't know how to do it, so Googal's written a rap about the **'y' to 'i' rule** to try to help him.

Googal's 'y' to 'i' Rap

If you spy with your little eye
A root word ending with the consonant 'y'
And you've a suffix you must add
Here's a rule that'll make you glad
Listen up, Deej, don't sulk and sigh
Just change that 'y' into an 'i'
Then add the suffix to the end
And you'll have a spelling that's right my friend.

Cheesy Chad says ...

If the root word ends in consonant 'y' and the suffix you want to add is 'ing', just add the suffix. So it's reply**ing** NOT repli**ing**

Words that end in the letter **'y'** must have the **'y'** changed to **'i'** before adding most suffixes:

lonely ▸ lonel**iness**   lazy ▸ laz**iest**   reply ▸ repl**ied**

7 Silence of the e's

Suffixes: Silent 'e'

Ulf's very quiet.

Yep, 'e's silent.

Ulf isn't talking, but that doesn't make him a **silent 'e'**. Unlike Ulf, a **silent 'e'** is a bit bossy. It doesn't say anything, but it makes the vowel that comes before it in a word sound like its alphabet name. For example, the **silent 'e'** in nice makes the 'i' that comes before it sound like its name. But if you add a suffix to a **silent 'e'** word then you remove the **silent 'e'** first. Let's try it and see:

Slic**e** – slicing

Rag**e** – raging

Oh yes it works – the **silent 'e'** has gone. If only there was a rule for making Mr Sumo go away!

Oi, I heard that!

Multiple Joyce

Which of these has a silent 'e'?

A globe
B frisbee
C ee aye addio
D Ee bah gum

The five vowels are: a,e,i,o,u.

In words that end with a **silent 'e'**, drop the 'e' when adding either a 'y' or a suffix that starts with a vowel:

rid**e** ▸ rid**ing**   nos**e** ▸ nos**y**

ag**e** ▸ ag**ing**   fam**e** ▸ fam**ous**

Words Easily Confused

Mountain Rescue

(1) To hill and back

Max, Ulf and Flash are visiting Scotland. They decide to climb a mountain.

You need to learn the spellings of the words in bold:

They **were** sad   **Whether** or not

Where is it?   Sunny **weather**

② A quick peak

Luckily they made it to the top, above the clouds where the sun is shining.

Easily confused:
breath/
breathe

Flash! How did you get here?

And how come you're not out of **breath**? I can hardly **breathe** after all that climbing.

Well, you two were going a bit slowly for me so I ran to the top. I've been up those two mountains too.

Joke Break

Jill: How do mountains hear?

Bill: With mountaineers, of course.

Watch out for **breath** and **breathe**:
We **breathe** air. Shagpile's **breath** pongs sometimes.

③ Well bread

Max, Ulf and Flash decide to have their lunch on the mountaintop.

Easily confused: brought/ bought

Where are the sandwiches? Did you bring them Max?

I thought you **brought** them, Flash. Didn't you buy the bread this morning?

Yes, I **bought** some bread from the shops this morning but I haven't **brought** the sandwiches with me. We'd better call Mountain Rescue – I'm starving. And to make things worse, who's that coming up the mountain?

Cheesy Chad says ...

Is last week's bring-and-buy sale called a brought-and-bought sale?

Brought and **bought** form the **past tense** of two different **verbs**:

bring ▶ **brought**   buy ▶ **bought**

4 High time

Max tries to call Mountain Rescue on her mobile …

Easily confused:
accept/
except

Please can you help us? We're stuck up a mountain with no lunch.

We cannot **accept** that as a reason to come out and rescue you **except** in instances where you are also being attacked by a large wrestler.

HELP!

HELP!

HELP!

Yikes! What will happen?

Accept and **except** are completely different:
Please **accept** this gift   It's free parking, **except** on Fridays.

YOU CAN DO IT!

⑤ Rescue rush

Phew! The kids are rescued just in time.

Easily confused:
cloth/clothes
metre/meter
idle/idol

Hey, we might be on the news!

That night they checked the TV listings to see when the news would be on.

7.00	The **Cloths** Show ✗
7.30	The 50 Greatest Parking **Metres** ✗
9.45	Rock **Idle** ✗
10.30	News

Wait a minute! There are three spelling mistakes there! It should say:

7.00	The **Clothes** Show ✓
7.30	The 50 Greatest Parking **Meters** ✓
9.45	Rock **Idol** ✓
10.30	News

Multiple Joyce

Which of these is dangerous?

A lightening
B lightning
C litening
D mashed potato

idol = something to worship   **idle** = lazy

clothes = what you wear   **cloth** = fabric

meter = a machine for measuring   **metre** = 100cm

Homophones
Lake It or Not?

1 All going swimmingly

It's a hot day. The gang decide to go swimming at a lake in the country.

 Homophones are words that sound the same but are spelt differently (and have different meanings). There are two pairs of **homophones** in bold below. Make sure you know which is which:

I'm feeling **bored**   A wooden **board**

I **hear** a noise   It's over **here**

2 Wood you risk it?

Deej and Wozza decide to explore the woods.

Homophones:
peace/piece
sure/shore

I've had enough of all this **peace** and quiet. I want a **piece** of the action.

Make **sure** you know your way back to the lake **shore**. And watch out for wild animals!

Oh yeah – all those killer voles and six-foot woodlice ... ha ha!

Peace of cake

 Learn these confusing spellings:

a **piece** of paper   some **peace** and quiet
are you **sure**?   the sea **shore**

③ Forest grump

Wozza and Deej are soon deep in the forest …

Homophones:
past/passed
new/knew

I think we're lost – we **passed** that tree stump at half **past** four, about two hours ago.

I thought you said you **knew** the way back. We'd better try a **new** path then.

Cheesy Chad says …

'Knew' is the past tense of 'know'. I knew that!

Look at the difference:

it's all in the **past**   she **passed** an exam
he **knew** it   I have **new** shoes

④ Bear behind

An hour later, Deej and Wozza are back at the tree stump again and, to make things worse, it's started to move!

Homophones:
bear/bare
saw/sore

Ouch! A **bear**! And it's clawed my bum – I've got a **bare** behind!

I thought I **saw** it move before. That'll be **sore** in the morning Deej – run!

Joke Break

Sue: What do you get if you cross a bear and a skunk?

Pru: Winnie the Poo.

Same sound, different words:

teddy **bear**	**bare** feet
sore throat	**saw** it in half

⑤ A load of pants

They finally get back to the lake.

Homophones:
caught/court
threw/through

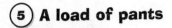

Deej! Where are your trousers? If you get **caught** without them you could end up in **court**!

I **threw** them away as we ran **through** the woods – a big *momma* killer bear was chasing us!

Oh sure ... a bear? We believe you ... snort!

Do you know how to spell these homophones?

caught out	tennis **court**
threw a wobbly	just passing **through**

YOU CAN DO IT!

⑥ Bear cheek

The gang are glad to be home, especially Deej.

Homophones:
paw/poor/pour
wood/would

Poor old Deej … he has **paw** marks on his botty. Better **pour** him a nice cup of tea.

Well, he **would** go into the **wood**, wouldn't he!

Multiple Joyce

Which of these are homophones?

A one/won
B two/lost
C three/icicle
D homophone/mobile phone

Make sure you know these words:

dog's **paw**   **poor** old me   **pour** with rain

carve **wood**   you **would**

Syllables
Break It Up

Syllables:
Individual beats

① Sound it out

Ulf gives a long word the chop.

Syllables are the individual beats in a word. The word 'lum-ber-jack' has three beats, or syllables. He'd better take care, or he'll end up in hos-pit-al.

Every word is made up of one or more syllables:

Goo-gal   Shag-pile   Su-mo   Woz-za

2 Hunt the syllable

Ulf finds spelling a bit of a monster.

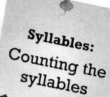

Syllables:
Counting the
syllables

Ulf..how do you spell dinosaur?

Dynosaw.

That's not how the dictionary spells it.

She didn't ask him how the dictionary spells it.

Ulf is writing a letter to the Dinosaur Appreciation Society but he can't spell the word 'lizard'. And he doesn't know how to break the word down into syllables. Googal tells him to count the vowel sounds, because each syllable must have a vowel sound. Lizard has two **vowels** ('i' and 'a') which means it has two syllables: l**i**z-**a**rd. Ulf spells each of these and then puts them together to make lizard!

Cheesy Chad says ...

If there are two vowels together, only count them as one vowel, e.g. keep and dinos**au**r.

Each syllable must have a **vowel** or a **vowel sound**, so **count the vowels** or **vowel sounds** to find the number of syllables in a word:

c**a**t (1)   s**u**p**e**r (2)   r**e**m**e**mb**e**rs (3)   d**i**n**o**s**au**r (3)

③ Break it down

Googal and Ulf see an elephant at the zoo.

> Syllables:
> Make words easier to spell

> I'm going to write an essay on an elephant.

> Wow! Then you're going to need a really big ladder.

> My elephant's sick. Do you know a good animal doctor?

Googal tells Ulf that elephants never forget anything because they have terrific memories. Ulf's impressed. He wants to know if an elephant can remember how to spell 'elephant'. Googal reminds Ulf that the best way to spell a long word like elephant is to sound out the syllables and then spell them. Elephant has three syllables so it becomes **e**-le-ph**a**nt.

> No. All the doctors I know are people.

Breaking words down into **syllables** makes them **easier** to **spell**:

pr**o**b-l**e**m   n**o**w-**a**-days   v**e**-g**e**-ta-bl**e**

(4) Vote for Sumo

Mr Sumo gives a speech.

Syllables:
Open
syllables

Mr Sumo is giving a speech and Googal has got the job of reporting it for the school newspaper. Mr Sumo is showing off by using lots of fancy words like 'portfolio' and 'status quo'. This doesn't upset Googal – she knows that the vowel at the end of an **open** syllable sounds like its name, so she uses this to help her spell the words.

An **open syllable** is one that ends with a vowel. In an **open syllable** the vowel sound at the end of the syllable is long and sounds like its name:

G**o**   w**e**   **pa**–per   n**o**   **ta**–ble   **ti**–ger

⑤ On the fast track

Flash meets her hero.

Syllables:
Closed
syllables

What do you call a sweater on a mountain top?

A high jumper.

Flash is meeting her hero, the world champion athlete, Ima De Best. But Flash is too bashful to speak. Bashful has two **closed syllables**, bash–ful. Both end with a consonant, so the vowels don't sound like their names. You need to remember this when trying to spell words with **closed syllables**. The vowels are a bit like Flash – too shy to speak up.

Joke Break

Q: What starts with 'e', ends with 'e' and only has one letter?

A: An envelope.

A **closed syllable** is one that ends in a consonant. In a closed syllable, the vowel sound is short and doesn't sound like its name:

rab-bit   ran   gun   pot   sup-per

6 Here comes the sun

Max and Wozza catch some rays.

Syllables:
Learning
syllables

What do you call a snowman with a suntan?

A puddle.

Max has a notion that her devotion to suntan lotion will set in motion the proper protection for her skin. She's learned it's bad to get burned.

As you can see in Wozza's diary, the same **syllables** can often appear in different words. This means if you **learn** the **syllable** in one word you can use it to help you spell other words in which it appears. For example: It's not the best feel**ing** to be red and peel**ing**.

Multiple Joyce

Which of these words has three syllables?

A Day break
B Daisy Daisy
C Wednesday
D Day off

Some syllables like '**ment**', '**ing**' and '**ly**' are found in lots of different words:

pay**ment**   agree**ment**   try**ing**   kiss**ing**   slow**ly**   sad**ly**

Look-say-cover-write-check

Daffy Café

Look-say-cover-write-check
A way to learn spellings

1 The blackboard bungle

Ulf has landed a job in a greasy spoon café, the House of Lards.
His job is to write the specials on the blackboard each day.
Googal goes to check how he's getting on …

Look-say-cover-write-check is a useful method for **learning** the spellings of words you have been given or need to know.

43

2) It's no yolk!

That evening, Googal helps Ulf to learn the menu for the next day.

Look-say-cover-write-check:
First look at the word

Ok, Ulf, the starter tomorrow is scrambled eggs. Let's try to learn the word 'scrambled'.

Hang on, I can't spell egg yet.

Googal tells Ulf that first he needs to **look** at the word carefully.

Joke Break

Ned: How do you know squirrels are smarter than chickens?

Ted: Well, I've never seen Kentucky fried squirrel.

The first stage of learning a word is to **look** at it carefully. Try to notice three things:

the **shape**   the **letter patterns**   any **sounds**

3) I say, I say

Ulf is trying to learn the word 'scrambled' and he's doing well.

Look-say-cover-write-check:
Say the word

Ok, Ulf, you've looked at the word. Next you must say it.

It.

No, Ulf, the word is 'scrambled'.

Oh no – we'd better put it back together then.

Cheesy Chad says ...

Remember, some words aren't spelt the way they sound and some don't sound the way the way they're spelt!

To learn a word, first look at it carefully then **say** it (sounding each part carefully if it helps):
Scr-am-ble-d

4 Big foot

Googal is determined to help Ulf learn the word 'scrambled'.

Look-say-cover-write-check:
Cover the word

> Right, Ulf, you've looked at the word, and said scrambled (finally), now you must cover it up.

> Ok – I'll use this handy anvil.

> Ulf, I think you've covered my foot as well!

Handsome six-footer

After looking at the word and saying it, the next stage is to **cover** it up so you can't copy.

Use something lighter than an anvil …

5 **Write or rong?**

Ulf feels that this might just work, and his confidence is high.

> Right, Ulf, next you must write the word.

> Ok – how do you spell it?

Here's Ulf's effort:

scramblek

After look-say-cover, you **write** the word, trying hard to remember:

the **shape**   **letter patterns**   **sounds**

47

⑥ Check book

Ulf is excited that he's finally learning to spell a word.

Look-say-cover-write-check:
Check the word

Ok, Ulf, now compare your spelling and the word 'scrambled'.

Scrambled

Scramblek

Mine's better. Hang on, this d at the end is wrong!

No, your k is wrong, but you came very close. Now you must try again: look-say-cover-write-check.

Multiple Joyce

Which of these will help you to learn spellings?

A Look-say-cover-write-chips
B Stare-shout-duvet-scribble-choc
C Look-say-cover-write-check
D Panic-run-jump-explode

After writing a word, the last part is to **check** it very carefully to see if it's right. If not, have another go.

Letter Patterns
Mr Sumo's Menagerie

1 Mixed up confusion

Letter patterns:
Sets of
letters

Mr Sumo likes to keep unusual pets.

Mr Sumo has a pas**sion** for keeping peculiar pets he's seen on televi**sion**. He makes a deci**sion** to give himself permis**sion** to go on a mis**sion** to buy some more and bring them back to his man**sion**. But then he hears an explo**sion** from his garden.

Mr Sumo's two pet rhinos have been in a colli**sion** and are suffering from concus**sion**!

Cheesy Chad says ...

Learning a letter pattern like '**sion**' can help you spell lots of words that use that use that letter pattern.

Letter patterns are **sets of letters** that are often found together in English words:

ing   **tion**   **ight**   **ieve**   **ound**

② **Proceed with caution**

Mr Sumo's pets keep him hanging around.

Mr Sumo has to take ac**tion**. He grabs a bottle of 'Rhino headache lo**tion**' and pours the po**tion** on the bumps on the rhinos' heads. This causes a commo**tion** and sets the rhinos in mo**tion**. They chase Mr Sumo all over his garden until he scrambles up a tree.

 If you learn how to spell a letter pattern like '**tion**' you can use it to spell lots of different words that have the same letter pattern:

sta**tion**   promo**tion**   no**tion**   locomo**tion**

(3) Caught on the horns of a dilemma

The rhinos want to make a couple of points to Mr Sumo.

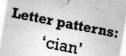

Letter patterns: 'cian'

You don't need a die**tician** to tell you that Mr Sumo is too heavy to hang from the tree branch for long. And Mr Sumo doesn't need an opti**cian** to tell him that those rhino horns are very sharp. A mathemati**cian** might point out that two angry rhinos are twice as bad as one angry rhino, but Mr Sumo already knows that. What he needs is a magi**cian** to make the rhinos disappear – otherwise he'll soon need a physi**cian**!

Joke Break

Child: Dad, Mum's fighting with a grizzly bear in the garden!

Dad: Don't panic, son. I'm sure the bear will be able to take care of itself.

The letters '**cian**' are a common letter pattern. It is used when spelling a word that describes a person's job:

musi**cian**   politi**cian**   electri**cian**

YOU CAN DO IT!

④ The human pyramid

The Odd Mob hear a frantic cry for help.

Letter patterns: 'ould'

The Odd Mob is hurrying past Mr Sumo's house when they hear him call for help. They want to go home to scoff a large bag of jam doughnuts they've just bought, but they know they sh**ould** stop and help. And they w**ould** if they c**ould**, but the garden wall is too high for them to climb over. Ulf stands on a m**ould**y b**ould**er, but it's not high enough. Then Googal has a brainwave. She tells the Odd Mob to make a human pyramid. She climbs up on their sh**ould**ers and peers over the top of the wall

Cheesy Chad says ...

Remember, some letter patterns look the same but don't sound the same, eg mould, should, could.

Here are more examples of words spelt using the '**ould**' letter pattern:

m**ould**   sh**ould**n't   w**ould**n't   c**ould**n't

⑤ A jammy escape

Googal has a sweet solution to save Mr Sumo.

Googal can see that the b**ough** Mr Sumo's hanging on to is about to break. She knows it's going to be a t**ough** job trying to save him, th**ough** she's determined to try. She gets the gang to pass her up the bag of jam d**ough**nuts. Then Googal c**ough**s to attract the rhinos' attention. They trot over to her and she throws down the d**ough**nuts. She's done en**ough**. The large beasts forget all about Mr Sumo and while they're gobbling up the goodies, he drops down on to the r**ough** grass beneath the tree and makes his escape.

Joke Break

Teacher: How do you stop a shark from smelling you?

Deej: Put a clothes peg on its nose!

Use the '**ough**' letter pattern to spell words like:

r**ough**ly   t**ough**er   c**ough**ing

6 The hound of the Sumos

Letter patterns: 'ound'

Mr Sumo is feeling hounded.

Mr Sumo's troubles aren't over. Before he can reach the safety of his mansion he hears a s**ound** behind him. He turns to see his two-headed vampire h**ound** is on the loose from its p**ound**. It has its noses to the gr**ound** and has f**ound** Mr Sumo's scent. The h**ound** comes b**ound**ing after him! Mr Sumo thinks he's done for but is ast**ound**ed when the h**ound** just gives him a great big lick with both its tongues. Luckily for Mr Sumo it's a vegetarian vampire h**ound** and only eats blood oranges.

Use the '**ound**' letter pattern to spell words like:

r**ound**   reb**ound**   m**ound**

⑦ **Too hot to handle**

Mr Sumo is grateful to the Odd Mob for saving him from the rhinos, so he invites them into his mansion to show them his collection of peculiar pets.

Mr Sumo takes the Odd Mob down into a cellar that is as black as n**ight**. He turns on the l**ight** and a terrifying s**ight** gives them a fr**ight**. The cellar is home to a bottom-faced fire belcher. It objects to being disturbed and it wants to f**ight**! The Odd Mob take fl**ight** before it can burn their bottoms!

Joke Break

Q: Why shouldn't you take an elephant to the zoo?

A: Because it would rather go to the cinema.

Use the **'ight'** letter pattern to spell words like:

r**ight**   **tigh**ten   m**igh**ty   he**ight**

⑧ I don't believe it

Ulf upsets Mr Sumo but it isn't his fault, honest.

Letter patterns: 'ieve'

When Mr Sumo sees one of his prized Peruvian wobble wifflers poking its head out of Ulf's pocket, he accuses the Odd Mob of being th**ieve**s. He won't bel**ieve** that the wobble wiffler had run up Ulf's trouser leg before Ulf could stop it. He retr**ieve**s his pet and then orders the Odd Mob out of his mansion.

The Odd Mob are cross with Mr Sumo for calling them fibbers and for not letting them see the rest of his pets, but I don't expect they'll gr**ieve** for too long. After all, the most peculiar thing in Mr Sumo's collection is Mr Sumo himself and the Odd Mob see more than enough of him.

Multiple Joyce

Which of these has an 'ough' letter pattern?

A knitting pattern
B tartan pattern
C tie-dye pattern
D enough patterns

Use the '**ieve**' letter pattern to spell words like:
bel**ieve**   s**ieve**   ach**ieve**ment   retr**ieve**r

Plurals
Lots of Them About

Plurals:
Add an 's'

1) A testing time

The Odd Mob need somewhere to sit and study.

I like to listen to really loud music when I'm on my own.

I'd hate to be with you when you're on your own.

The Odd Mob have got to sit down quietly and study for a test at school, but they've only one book, one table and one chair between them. They're stuck. Then Googal comes up with a brilliant idea. She **adds an 's'** to the book, the table and the chair, which turns them from singular into plural. So now the Odd Mob have all the book**s**, table**s** and chair**s** they need.

Cheesy Chad says ...

'Singular' means one of something. 'Plural' means more than one.

For most English words just **add an 's'** to the end of the word to make it plural:

dog ▸ dog**s**   hat ▸ hat**s**   fact ▸ fact**s**

② A sign of the times

Mr Sumo breaks the rules.

Mr Sumo's got himself a job as a signwriter. But he won't stick to the rules and he's giving all the words that end in 'y' the wrong plural. It's causing chaos. So it's up to the Odd Mob to stop him.

Luckily they know that if a word has a consonant before the 'y' then the plural is 'ies'. But if it has a vowel before the 'y' then you just add an 's'.

They save the **day** but it won't be many more **days** before Mr Sumo thinks up another evil **plan** (or **plans**) to cause mischief.

Cheesy Chad says ...

Remember the difference between a **vowel** and a **consonant**. The vowels are 'a', 'e', 'i', 'o' and 'u'. All the other letters are consonants.

If the word has a **consonant** before the final '**y**' then the plural ends with '**ies**':

try ▸ tr**ies**   stor**y** ▸ stor**ies**

If the word has a **vowel** before the final '**y**' just add an '**s**':

donk**ey** ▸ donkey**s**   play ▸ play**s**

3 Things that go bump in the night

Googal writes a poem.

Googal's written a poem using lots of words that have 'es' as their plural. But she's cheated on one ending – can you see which one? (BIG CLUE – it's 'loxes')

The Ghastly Gathering

Two geniu**ses** were washing up di**shes**
As lightning fla**shes** scorched and lit up the sky.
They heard fo**xes** barking, looked out the window
And saw ma**sses** of wit**ches** dance by.
Giants threw pun**ches** while goblins with hun**ches**
Ate sandwi**ches**, and toad and frog pie.
Orcs drank from wine gla**sses** while moonlight glittered
In the iri**ses** of cruel vampires' eyes.

They'd heard all about hoa**xes** and midnight jin**xes**
But this was no joke to be scorned
So they found some large bo**xes** with strong iron lo**xes**
And hid safely inside them 'til dawn.

To make words that end with 'x', 'sh', 's', 'ss', and 'ch' into plurals just add '**es**':

bo**x** ▶ bo**xes**   bu**sh** ▶ bush**es**   atla**s** ▶ atlas**es**
gla**ss** ▶ glass**es**   chur**ch** ▶ chur**ches**

4 It's only a game

The Odd Mob play football.

Plurals:
Words ending in 'f' or 'fe'

Football is boring. Get a life, err... lives.

Wozza, Deej, Max, HMD, Googal and Ulf are playing Flash at football. In the first **half** the gang scores one goal (it was a rebound off Ulf's bottom), but Flash doesn't score any. She's forgotten her boots and has to go home to get them. In the second **half**, Flash is back and scores 100 goals. It really is a game of two hal**ves**.

Joke Break

Q: Why should babies play football?

A: Because they're great at dribbling!

When a word ends in '**f**' or '**fe**' you usually change the '**f**' or '**fe**' to '**v**' before adding '**es**':

lea**f** ▸ lea**ves**   hal**f** ▸ hal**ves**   kni**fe** ▸ kni**ves**

⑤ What a hero

Mr Sumo shows off his muscles.

Plurals:
Nouns that end in 'o'

Mr Sumo thinks he's got muscles like the her**oes** from Ancient Greece. So he's entered a body-building contest. Most people think his head and body look like two potat**oes** on legs. Somebody throws a tomat**o** at him – then everybody joins in. This is unkind because the tomat**oes** are still in their tins!

Multiple Joyce

Which of these plurals is correct?

A Shirtes
B Vestes
C Sockes
D Shoes

Most **nouns that end in 'o'** can be made into plurals by adding 'es':

potato ▸ potato**es**   tomato ▸ tomato**es**   hero ▸ hero**es**

Silent Letters
The Sumo Story!

Silent letters:
Silent
'w'

1 Mystery man

Mr Sumo is the mortal enemy of the gang. But who is he and how did he become their enemy? This section will tell all ...

Mr Sumo is a heavyweight **w**restler. He is so flabby that he can **w**riggle the **w**rinkles on his **w**rists.

Wrestler, **w**riggle, **w**rinkle and **w**rist are all **silent 'w'** words, which means you don't say the 'w'.

Wrap music

Watch out for these **silent 'w'** words too:

wreck   **wr**ong   **wh**ole   **tw**o

A **silent 'w'** is often followed by the letter **'r'**:

writing   **wr**estle   **wr**ote

② Toffee trouble

How did Mr Sumo get to be that large?

Silent letters:
Silent
'c'

Mr Sumo wanted big muscles, so he studied science and joined a gym. He was disciplined about his exercises.

But one day he opened a packet of toffee sauce with some scissors. The scent was lovely – and so was the taste …

Mr Sumo couldn't stop eating it – his descent into flab began.

Cheesy Chad says …

Science, scene and scissors all have a **silent 'c'**.

A **silent 'c'** is usually found after the letter **'s'**:

muscle   scenery   discipline

③ Knife knowledge

One day, Ulf borrowed Mr Sumo's best camping knife and lost it. Whoops.

> **Silent letters:**
> Silent 'k'

Mr Sumo was not too pleased …

> I'll knock your block off! I'll knot your knees together with the knickers your granny knitted! And I know who your friends are!

Ulf knew that he was in trouble, so he ran away. From that day on, Mr Sumo and the gang did <u>not</u> get along.

Killer silent 'k' wordsearch

K	N	A	C	K
X	Z	Q	Z	Q
Z	Q	X	X	Z
Q	X	Z	Q	Z
K	N	O	W	N

Nasty! Did you notice all those **silent 'k'** words Mr Sumo used? Do you **k**now any more?

A **silent 'k'** always goes with the letter 'n':

knight   **kn**eeling   un**kn**own

④ How annoying!

From that moment onwards, Mr Sumo began to annoy the gang.

He hurt HMD's thum**b** with a com**b**.

Then he disguised himself as a plum**b**er, so he could drop crum**b**s all over Max's bathroom.

Joke Break

Ron: What do you get if you cross a cow, a sheep and a goat?

Don: The milky baa kid!

And after that he climbed a tom**b** to bom**b** the gang with toy lam**b**s!

Take a look at all those **silent 'b'** words. Notice anything? Here are two more:

de**b**t   dou**b**t

A **silent 'b'** is often found after the letter '**m**':

nu**mb**   cli**mb**er   bo**mb**ing

⑤ Royal writers

The gang were so cross that they wrote to the Queen to complain about Mr Sumo.

Silent letters:
Silent 'g'

Dear Your Majesty,

We are fed up because Mr Sumo is really getting on our nerves. He broke the garden gnome that Flash designed, he gnashes his yucky teeth at us and he keeps following us, even on foreign holidays!

We want him to resign from his silly campaign of annoying our gang.

We hope you can help us, since you reign over the country.

Signed,

Googal, Deej, Max, Ulf, Flash, Wozza, HMD

PS. Please behead him or lock him in a smelly dungeon, ta.

Unfortunately, the Queen didn't help them, although she did send eight chocolate corgis ...

How many **silent 'g'** words are in the letter?

A **silent 'g'** goes together with the letter '**n**':

si**gn**   **gn**arled   desi**gn**er

(6) On guard!

So, the gang just have to keep as far away
from Mr Sumo as they can. But it's not easy …

HMD must g**u**ard
his g**u**itars from
g**u**ilty-looking
g**u**ests at his house.

Silent 'u' often goes with '**g**': **gu**ess, ton**gu**e, **gu**ardian

Max checks her dad's ve**h**icle
every **h**our for someone
who's not **h**onest.

Silent 'h' often goes with '**o**': **h**onestly, **h**onour, **h**ourly

Googal won't wa**l**k or ta**l**k
with fo**l**k who are six and a
ha**l**f times bigger than her.

Silent 'l' often goes with '**k**', '**m**' or '**f**': cha**l**k, pa**l**m, ca**l**f.

YOU CAN DO IT!

(7) Hopeless hobbies

So, apart from annoying the gang, what else does Mr Sumo get up to?

Silent letters:
Silent
'n', 'p', 's', 't'

Every autumn, he sings hymns on top of a column.

He collects receipts for raspberry yoghurts, which he keeps in a cupboard.

He takes holidays on a very small island called the Isle of Mite.

He often listens to the rustle of leaves near the castle where he wrestles.

Multiple Joyce

Which of these is a real bird?

A wrobin
B wcrow
C wren
D wBoeing 747

Silent 'n' is found after 'm': hymn, condemn
Silent 'p' moves about: receipt, psychology
Silent 's' is rare indeed: island, isle
Silent 't' often goes with 's': hustle, fasten

68

Tricky Words
Freaky Film Fest!

① On your bike

It's raining outside, so the gang have gone to the local multi-screen cinema. Nearly everyone wants to see a different film, so they split up.

Googal goes to see the arty low-budget film 'Cyclo' ...

What was the film about, Googal?

Well, one **autumn**, a young **secretary** leaves **college** and **decides** to start up a **business** selling **bicycles** to **religious** women. It's **definitely** **different** ...

Mmm ... I don't think I'll bother seeing that one. Anyway, watch out for the tricky spellings in bold. Cheesy Chad has a tip for remembering them.

Cheesy Chad says ...

Saying each part of a tricky word carefully can help you to spell it, e.g. bus-i-ness, re-lig-i-ous.

Watch out for **letters** that are easily missed:
diff**e**rent   autum**n**   religi**o**us

YOU CAN DO IT!

② The cold hole

Deej goes to see the tense disaster movie
'The Cold Hole' ...

Tricky words:
**Double
letters**

What happened in your film then, Deej?

Right. A **beautiful professor** is exploring the **Arctic** all alone when there is a terrible **accident** and she **disappears** down a hole in the ice. It's **February** and the **temperature** drops to minus 89°. There doesn't seem to be any hope when, suddenly, a **vehicle** appears from nowhere. Sadly the vehicle falls down the hole too and they all die.

Can you spell all the words that Deej says in bold? They're not easy! One way to get them right is to **learn them** using the look-say-cover-write-check method (see pages 43–48).

Joke Break

Q. What has a bottom at the top?

A: Your legs.

Watch out for **double letters** in some words:
profe**ss**or   a**cc**ident   disa**pp**ear

(3) Night of the killer carrot

Wozza goes to see a scary adventure film.

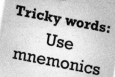

Tricky words:
Use
mnemonics

Tell me all about the film, Woz.

It was really **interesting**. A **passenger** on a jet has a nasty **surprise** when he is attacked by a **vicious vegetable** from his in-flight meal. Everyone is overpowered by the carrot, **except** a **family** of **eight** midgets who tie it up and **guard** it **until** the plane lands. Tom Cruise played the carrot.

Loads of people have trouble spelling the 10 words in bold above. So, how can you remember them? One way is to use **mnemonics**, for example:

Most gu**ard**s are '**ard**!

There is more about mnemonics on pages 88–92.

Keep an eye out for **letters** you **don't** need to **say**:

int**e**resting   su**r**prise   veg**e**table   fam**i**ly

YOU CAN DO IT!

④ View to a queue

HMD decides to see a new action thriller.

Tricky words: Pinpoint the problem letters

Was it as good as you hoped, HMD?

This film was all-action, sister! An **author** visits her local **library** to find some **information** about **calendars**. She has to **queue quietly** for a book that is **necessary** for her research. She waits 20 **minutes** then is told to come back **tomorrow**. Awesome!

HMD has no taste in films, but he can spell all the hard words he used in his description. He does it by remembering the tricky bits in each word, for example:

calend**ar**, ne**cess**ary, min**u**te.

Pet shop

Try to learn where **problem letters** go:

li**br**ary   to**morr**ow   auth**or**   q **ue ue**

72

⑤ Double oh no

Max is desperate to see the latest Bond film.

Tricky words:
Look for root
words

What was the plot then, Max?

Well, a **weird** villain tells the British **Government** that he will destroy the **environment** around Rotherham unless they can **guess** his **favourite colour**. Bond finds his **address** using the phone book then, disguised as an **ordinary** but **humorous** henchman, blows everything up.

Cheesy Chad says ...

Watch out! There is no root word for 'weird' and the root word of 'humorous' is 'humour'.

Well, no surprises there. But what about these nine tricky spellings? Sometimes it helps if you know the **root word** of a spelling, for example:

government – root word: govern
favourite – root word: favour

Watch out for root words that give you spelling clues:

different   **secret**ary   dis**appear**

73

YOU CAN DO IT!

6 Complete mystery

Ulf went to see a mystery film. At least, that's what it turned out to be ...

How good was it, Ulf?

This is **probably** the best movie since Star Warts. It's difficult to **describe** but the **beginning** is very **similar** to Narnia, the middle is a **separate** story about pies and the end is an **unusual** but **skilful** action scene featuring lots of yoghurt. In my **opinion**, it's **excellent** ... ok, I admit it – I slept through the whole film.

What a wally! But anyway, there are some nasty spellings in his description and they're all words you need to know. Sometimes, thinking about **prefixes** and **suffixes** (see pages 13–25) can help, for example:

describe, **un**usual, skil**ful**, excell**ent**.

By the way – Flash never did get to see a film. I wonder why?

Multiple Joyce

Which of these words has a correct suffix?

A busipooo
B busiwizzi
C business
D busibee

Prefixes and suffixes are letter patterns at the beginning and end of words:

reappear   **bi**cycle   informa**tion**   vici**ous**

74

Useful Rules
The Spelling Bee

1 A friend in need

Max to the rescue.

Your honey or your life!

Oh, do bee-hive yourself, Spider.

Max rescues a bee from a spider's web. To her amazement it turns out to be a Spelling Bee. In return for Max's kindness, the bee shares its spelling secrets with her.

First up it tells her its favourite spelling rule: **'i before e except after c'**. The bee says that it's the least it can do for a **friend** in need and Max is delighted to **receive** this tip.

Cheesy Chad says ...

There are a few exceptions to this rule, like **weird** and **science**, for instance.

If a word makes a long 'e' sound remember it's **'i' before 'e' except after 'c'**:

chief	brief	field	shield
receive	ceiling	deceit	receipt

75

② The weight watcher

Useful rules:
'e' before 'i'

Mr Sumo goes on a diet.

Mr Sumo's too heavy for his h**ei**ght so he's been trying to lose w**ei**ght. He's been on a diet for **ei**ght weeks. It isn't working.

Here's your double cheeseburger and chips.

Thanks. And I'll have a slim-line water as I'm on a diet.

The Spelling Bee doesn't have a rule to help Mr Sumo get slim, but she does tell Max that if words have an 'ay' sound like w**ei**gh, or an 'eye' sound like h**ei**ght, then the rule is to put the **'e' before 'i'** when spelling them.

What's more dangerous than being with a fool?

Fooling with a bee.

If a word has an 'ay' or an 'eye' sound, the rule is to put the **'e' before the 'i'**:

eight   w**ei**ght   h**ei**ght   n**ei**ghbour

3 Can or cane?

Ulf's in a muddle.

Useful rules:
Silent 'e'
makes a vowel
say its name

This is a mate for you to sleep on.

But I want a mat not a mate.

Ulf keeps messing up. He wanted to put some t**ape** on his book but somehow he put a tap on it. Then he put a c**ape** on his head instead of his cap and walked into a wall because he couldn't see anything.

This can't go on, so Max lends him her Spelling Bee. The Bee tells Ulf that if a vowel in a short word like 'pine' sounds like its name, it ends with a **silent 'e'**. This is important because there's a big difference between a pin and a pine. But by remembering this rule, Ulf can stop muddling up his spellings and start getting the right words.

A **silent 'e'** at the end of a word makes the vowel in front sound like its name:

b**a**ke   c**o**ncret**e**   sid**e**   h**o**m**e**   flum**e**

(4) To bee or not to bee?

Wozza is upset with Max's Spelling Bee.

Useful rules:
Drop the silent 'e'

Do you like my Spelling Bee?

No, it's bee-witched you.

Wozza and Max are arguing about how to spell arguing. Wozza says it's spelled 'argueing', but Max says it's spelled 'arguing'. She bets Wozza £1 she's right. Max is, but she cheated. The Spelling Bee told her to **drop the silent 'e'** because the ending 'ing' begins with a vowel. Wozza's so cross she tells the Spelling Bee to buzz off!

Joke Break

Q. Why do bees have sticky hair?

A: Because they use honey combs.

The five vowels are: a, e, i, o, u.

When you add an ending to a word that ends with a **silent 'e'**, drop the **silent 'e'** if the ending begins with a vowel, e.g.

surpris**e** – surpris**ing**   blam**e** – blam**ing**

⑤ Pay attention

Max has written a story about how the Spelling Bee became magical.

Useful rules:
The 'shun'
sound

How the Spelling Bee Became Magical
by
Max

One day a bee saw a magician with a fierce expression who was making a potion while musicians stood to attention and played magical music with a passion. At the end of this session he had a notion to wash the bee in the lotion and Hey Presto the bee turned into a Spelling Bee.

Max has stuck to the rules about words that make a **'shun' sound**:

Use '**sion**' for words that end in 's' or 'd'.

Use '**cian**' for words that are about people.

Use '**tion**' for all other words that end in a **shun** sound.

Use '**sion**' if the root word ends in 's' or 'd':

extend – exten**sion**   express – expres**sion**

Use 'cian' if the root word is about people: musician

Use '**tion**' for all other 'shun' words: mo**tion**   po**tion**

⑥ Snakes alive

Mr Sumo is a slippery character.

Useful rules:
Double 'f',
'l' and 's'

There's a snake on your windscreen, Mr Sumo.

Yes, it's a windscreen viper.

Cheesy Chad says ...

Mr Sumo wants to be careful – that snake's bite may be worse than its hiss. But the Spelling Bee isn't being hiss-terical when she tells Max that short words that end in '**f**', '**l**' or '**s**' normally end in double letters.

Remember, each beat in a word is a syllable. For example, 'dog' has one beat so it has one syllable but 'Shagpile' has two beats so it has two syllables.

Words of one syllable that end with the sound '**f**', '**l**' or '**s**' usually end in double letters:

cli**ff**   flu**ff**   hi**ll**   wi**ll**   to**ss**   dre**ss**

⑦ **Something's buzzing**

The Spelling Bee is in demand.

We want a buzzword with you.

Phew! It's getting a bit swarm out here.

There's a **qu**eue of bees lining up to **qu**iz the Spelling Bee. They've been on a **qu**est to find her. The **Qu**een Bee wants her back at the hive. They keep droning on about how the **Qu**een Bee's doing a crossword and she needs help to answer the **qu**estions.

Max listens to the buzzing bees and hears another spelling rule: that the letters **'q' and 'u' always go together**.

'**Qu**' is a pair. Q is never written on its own, e.g.

quack   **qu**ote   **qu**it   **qu**iet   **qu**ite   **qu**iz   **qu**ick

8 To have and have not

Max and the Spelling Bee say goodbye.

I've got to make a bee-line for home.

You can catch a buzz at the buzz stop.

Useful rules: Use 've' at the end of words with a 'v' sound

It's time for the Spelling Bee to go but she tells Max one last spelling rule before she flies off. She says that English words hardly ever end in 'v', so use '**ve**' to spell words that end with a 'v' sound. Max thanks her for her help and tells her to hi**ve** a nice day.

Multiple Joyce

Which of these is a spelling rule?

A Rule Britannia
B Rule of thumb
C Sumo rules ok
D i before e

English words that sound like they end in '**v**' nearly always end in '**ve**':

ner**ve**	sa**ve**	ha**ve**	bra**ve**
sla**ve**	li**ve**	di**ve**	hea**ve**

Compound Words
What Are the Odd Mob Up To?

(1) I can't believe it's not an insect

Ulf makes a mess.

Why are you putting wings on that butter, Ulf?

I'm making a butterfly.

A **compound word** is made when two smaller words are put together to make a new word. For example, if you put the words **butter** and **fly** together you get **butterfly**. Only don't try to do it like Ulf. If you do you won't get a compound word – you'll just get a mess.

Cheesy Chad says ...

Sometimes a compound word can have a very different meaning from the two words it's made of, e.g. lady + bird = ladybird.

A **compound word** is made when two words are joined together to form a new word:

news + paper = newspaper   eye + lid = eyelid

(2) Do it yourself

Deej builds Shagpile a new home.

Compound words:
Meaning

> Hey Shagpile, I've made a doghouse for you to sleep in.

> Thanks, but I'd rather sleep in a human house.

Sometimes you can work out the **meaning** of a compound word by looking at the two words that make it. For example, **dog** + **house** = **doghouse**. It's a house for dogs. But it's Deej who ends up in the doghouse when his dad finds out that Deej has used all the wood he'd bought to make new shelves for the kitchen. Deej can be a bit of a plank sometimes.

Joke Break

Q. What do you call a dog with no legs?

A: Anything you like – he still won't come.

You can often work out the **meaning** of a compound word by looking at what the two little words mean:

news + paper = newspaper
(a paper that has the news printed on it)

③ Send for the AA

Mr Sumo's going nowhere fast.

Compound words:
Breaking words down

Mr Sumo's car's had a breakdown

Is it an engine breakdown?

No, it's a nervous breakdown – have you seen the way Mr Sumo drives?

It's easier to spell compound words if you **break them down** into the words that make them, e.g.

Breakdown = break + down.

Joke Break

Q. What do you call a man with a car on his head?

A: Jack

Compound words that sound complicated are easier to spell if you **break them down**:

springtime = spring + time

④ Say what you see

Is Ulf going bonkers?

Compound words:
Say the words

You know what happens to people who talk to themselves.

Yes, they have a sensible conversation.

Ulf wants to smarten himself up, so he's writing to a scarecrow to ask if they can swap clothes. Wozza thinks Ulf is talking to himself, but really he's trying to spell the compound word: scarecrow. Ulf can hear that it's made up of two smaller words (scare + crow). He's **saying it slowly** to sound it out.

Multiple Joyce

Which of these is a compound word?

A ghost
B spook
C nightmare
D arghhh!

If you **sound out a compound word slowly**, you can hear that it's made up of two little words:

bedtime = bed + time

Mnemonics
Fashion Nonsense

1 Don't get shirty

The gang are doing a little clothes shopping in town.
Deej has found a shirt he likes.

Er,
why don't
you try it
on?

Oh, that
won't be nesess ...
nescess ... oh those
stupid c's and s's!

Oh dear, poor Deej can never
remember how to say or spell the
word **necessary**! He needs a
mnemonic – a memory jogger.

Here's a way to remember the c's
and s's in ne**c**e**ss**ary:

A shirt has **one c**ollar
and **two s**leeves.

Cheesy Chad says ...

Mnemonic has a
silent 'm' – say
'ne-mon-ic'.

A **mnemonic** is a way of **remembering** something:
de**ss**ert – **s**weet **s**tuff

YOU CAN DO IT!

② Going undie cover

Wozza and Flash need some new undies.
But why have they gone to the library?

Mnemonics:
Words within words

Finding a small word inside a
bigger word is a kind of mnemonic.
It's true – don't be**lie**ve a **lie**!

A pear of knickers

 Some **mnemonics** use words within words for the
tricky bits:

My **ma** knows her gram**ma**r

A good fri**end** stays to the **end**

③ **Jumbo gent**

HMD, Googal and Ulf are shopping for heavy metal wear.

Googal teaches HMD a mnemonic for remembering how to spell the word 'because':

> Because: big elephants can always understand small elephants.

Some spelling **mnemonics** work like acrostics, spelling out all of the letters of the word:

rhythm: **r**hythm **h**elps **y**our **t**wo **h**ips **m**ove

④ Retro kid

After nine hours shopping, Ulf still hasn't bought anything.

> Mnemonics:
> Make up your own

> I don't like patterns or plain or colour. I'm more into retro.

> Ulf, you're so retro you're Stone Age.

Googal is bored so she makes up a mnemonic for spelling the word 'colour':

Colour: **c**ome **o**n, **l**eave **o**ld **U**lf **r**etro.

Joke Break

Gav: Did you buy that sun cream in Boots?

Bav: No, I was wearing trainers.

 You can make up your own **mnemonics** for tricky words:

guard: **G**oogal's **u**tterances **a**re **r**arely **d**aft

(5) Fashion victims

At last, the Odd Mob have finished their clothes shopping.

It's great to be in a gang that **posesses** so much fashion sense.

You mean **posseses**?

He means **possessess**.

Actually, he means **possesses**. You can remember it with this rhyming mnemonic:

> Possesses possesses five s's

(Oh, and by the way, they have <u>no</u> fashion sense whatsoever).

Multiple Joyce

Which of these is a mnemonic for 'queue'?

A Double q, double m.
B Ue-ue spell queue you see.
C Thank Q.
D Never queue, just push in, do.

 Mnemonics that rhyme can sometimes help with spelling. Here's one for the tricky word '**address**':

Double 'd', double 's', is all you need to spell address.

Hidden Words
Watching the Detectives

Hidden words:
Words
within words

1 Breakout

The Odd Mob go looking for hidden words.

The school librarian, Dick Shunree, is worried. Words have been escaping from the books and are hiding in all sorts of places. If he can't find them he'll get the sack. So the Odd Mob help him track them down. Flash spots the first word '**get**' hiding in a sign at a ve**get**able stall in the market.

There's a **table** in the word vege**table** too!

Crikey, it must be a really big vegetable!

Some words are difficult to spell, so look for **hidden words** inside them. These will help remind you how to spell them:

'J**our**ney' has '**our**' hiding inside it.

② Word search

Shagpile smells a rat.

Hidden words:
Separate

> HMD, Deej and Shagpile are on the trail of a rat. This is a particularly dangerous word so they have to be very careful not to get bitten. Then Shagpile smells something! There's **a rat** hiding in the word 'sep**arat**e'.

Look out! There's a rat.

You're right! It's Mr Sumo.

Why are you late for school?

There are eight of us in my family but the alarm clock was set for seven.

If you remember that there's '**a rat**' in 'sep**arat**e' you will always spell the word separate correctly.

3 Can't see the word for the trees

Max and Wozza go word hunting in a wood.

Hidden Words: In tree names

Wozza and Max find lots of words hiding in the wood. There is a **chest** and a **nut** hiding in the **chestnut** tree, a **lane** in the p**lane** tree and an **arch** in the l**arch**. There's **more** in the syca**more**. They soon get tired of searching, so they leave the fo**rest** and go home for a **rest**.

Joke Break

Teacher. What grows on a palm tree?

Pupil: Fingers!

Here are some more examples of hidden words in trees:
b**loss**om = loss **bee**ch = bee br**an**ch = ran

4) At the zoo

Googal and Ulf go word searching at the zoo.

Hidden words:
In animal
names

Ulf and Googal are looking for hidden words at the zoo.
Ulf is trying to see if the kangaroo has got a word hidden in
its **pouch**. But it's a boxing
kangaroo so the only word
Ulf will find is '**Ouch**!'

Googal has more sense
than to go bothering the
animals so she has made
a list of the cr**eat**ures
she's found with hidden
words in them.

Words hiding in animals

Eleph**ant** = ant
Chimp**an**zee = pan
B**ear** = ear
Gazelle = gaze

You can find hidden words in animal names:
camel = came   mon**key** = key   **hip**po**pot**amus = hip, pot

(5) Who's hungry?

Mr Sumo goes looking for escaped words too, at an army base. Not a good choice …

Hidden words:
More examples

The soldiers be**lie**ve Mr Sumo is a spy, but he says there's a **lie** in that statement.

They want to **add** his **add**ress to their wanted list.

Mr Sumo says he can be g**one** in **one** minute.

The soldiers notice that mi**nut**e has a **nut** in it, and that nut is Mr Sumo!

They lock him in a **cell** – ex**cell**ent job, guys!

Joke Break

Teacher: What's the longest word in the dictionary?

Pupil: Smiles, 'cos there's a mile between the two s's.

Speaking of locking up, many tricky words have little words locked inside them:

fo**reign** – reign   **fat**her – fat   de**fin**ite – fin

⑥ A closed book

The Odd Mob have rounded up all the escaped words.

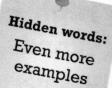

Hidden words:
Even more examples

Have you gone mad, Mr Librarian?

No! There are **words** hiding in these s**words**.

Dick Shunree, the school librarian's job is safe. He and the Odd Mob have found all the words that escaped. Now all he has to do is put the swords down without taking anyone's eye out!

Multiple Joyce

Which of these words is hiding a bee?

A Be off
B Behave
C Beetroot
D Behind

High Frequency Words

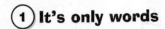
Writing a Book

High frequency words:
The words we use most

1) It's only words

Googal wants to write a book.

Googal wants the Odd Mob to write a book about themselves. She says they can each write one page, but Ulf says he doesn't know which words to use. Googal says there are over 600,000 English words he can choose from. Ulf reckons at the speed he writes it will take him at least a million years to use them all. Googal says he only needs to use a few words.

Oi! I want a word!

Fair enough - that still leaves 599,999 for the rest of us.

Although there are thousands of words in the English language, a small number of them appear again and again in the books we read. These words are called **high frequency words**.

Here are some high frequency words you need to know how to spell:

many   people   would   laugh   because

(2) Eat your words

Ulf does his best.

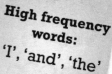

High frequency
words:
'I', 'and', 'the'

Ulf still can't make up his mind
which words to use. He could try
'**I**', '**and**' or '**the**', as these are
the high frequency words that
get used the most.

Ulf says he's going to write a
masterpiece but he'll probably
end up eating his words. He ate
a dictionary once. It didn't help
him improve his spelling but it
did help him find the meaning of
a new word – indigestion.

**Cheesy Chad
says ...**

It's a fact that
100 high
frequency words
make up half of
the words we
read.

'**I**', '**and**' and '**the**' are used ten times more often than
any other words.

③ Deej's story

Deej has a problem getting started on writing his page.

> **High frequency words:**
> Words with the same letter pattern

> I could write a story about myself. I should write a story about myself. I would write a story about myself – but I haven't got a pen.

The high frequency words **could**, **would** and **should** have the **same letter pattern: -ould**. If you learn the letter patterns in high frequency words it will help you remember how to spell them.

Other helpful letter patterns found in high frequency words are:

an – m**an**, m**an**y

ou – h**ou**se, **ou**r, **ou**t, y**ou**r

ow – h**ow**, n**ow**

pu – **pu**sh, **pu**ll, **pu**t

Cheesy Chad says ...

> Look for **parts of words** that are linked by meaning, e.g. 'Where is here? It's in there.'

 Learning the letter pattern can help you spell less common words with the **same letter pattern**:
sh**ould**er   b**ould**er

(4) Once a winner

Flash may be a good runner, but she's not so good at spelling.

High frequency words:
Make a word chain

I won every race on skool sports day. That is becoz I can run faster than other peepel. Anyone who thinks they can beat me is having a larf.

Flash has written her page but she's misspelled the words 'school', 'because', 'people' and 'laugh'. Googal can't help Flash run any quicker, but she can help her to spell. So she tells Flash to make a **chain of words**, where the first letter of each word in the chain is a letter from the word she wants to spell. Googal says the sillier the **word chain** the easier it is to remember how to spell the word. Flash comes up with:

School – **S**illy **c**hildren **h**op **o**ver **o**range **l**ollipops.

Because – **B**ig **e**agles **c**an **a**lways **u**se **s**ticky **e**nvelopes.

People – **P**eople **e**asily **o**ffend **p**oor **l**ittle **e**lves.

Joke Break

Now Flash is a top speller as well as a top runner!

Q. What do you get when a lorry full of tortoises crashes into a lorry full of terrapins?

A: A turtle disaster.

Making a word chain can help you remember how to spell high frequency words:

Laugh – **L**ittle **a**nts **u**ndermine **g**reat **h**ouses.

(5) Wozza needs a guide

Wozza's getting confused.

High frequency words:
Words that sound alike

> *Were all writing a book. Their are pictures two. There really good.*

Wozza doesn't know if she should use 'there' or 'their', 'too' or 'two' and 'were' or 'we're'. So Googal writes a guide to help Wozza remember the differences between these words.

GOOGAL'S GUIDE
We're is short for 'we are'.
Were is a past tense form of the verb 'be'.
Too means 'also', 'very' or 'over'.
Two means the number 2.
Their means it belongs to them.
There means that place (it's a place word, and so it contains the word '*here*').
They're is short for 'they are'.

Cheesy Chad says ...

> Words that sound alike but are spelt differently are called homophones, e.g. 'see' or 'sea'.

Some **words sound alike** but have different meanings and are spelt differently. You need to learn the differences so that you can spell them correctly:

you're (short for 'you are')　　**your** (it belongs to you)

(6) Cooking the books

Max bakes a fake cake.

High frequency words: Silent 'e'

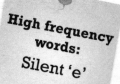

HOW TO BAKE A FAKE HOME MADE CAKE
By Max

Take cake mix. Put it in a tin, add water and shake it. Then bake it on a low flame in the oven. When the time is right, take it out and you've got a home made cake. Now all it needs is a name. (But if you make a mistake with your cake don't blame yourself and feel shame, just take a rake and bury it in the garden, mate!)

Max has written a recipe for her famous home-made cake. Well, it may be made with a shop-bought cake mix but at least she added the water at home.

Joke Break

Q. Which Shakespeare play is about a celebrity chef?

A: Ham Omelette.

If you remember that a **silent** 'e' helps the vowel before it sound like its name you will be able to spell lots of high frequency words:

came   home   make   name

(7) There's no rhyme or reason to it

HMD writes a song on his page.

Shagpile is a little dog
She only wants to **play**
She stole Mr Sumo's wig
And then she ran **away**.
You should have heard
The rude things Mr Sumo **said**
He didn't see where his hairpiece went
But he was seeing **red**.
Without his hairy wig
Mr Sumo looks a **fright**
So he won't come out in the day
He just comes out at **night**.

HMD wants to write a song about Shagpile and Mr Sumo to go on his page, so he's decided to rhyme some high frequency words.

Nearly half the words HMD's used in his song are high frequency words.

Multiple Joyce

Which of these isn't a high frequency word?

A And
B But
C So
D Fantabulous

Some high frequency words have rhyming patterns that will help you to **spell** other words that **rhyme** with them:
An**other** br**other** is a bit of a b**other**.

Common Letter Strings

Let's Make a Meal of It

1 Buried treasure!

One day, the gang hears a whole load of excited woofing ...

Shagpile, the gang's **hound**, **found** a **mound** of **pound** coins in Max's garden.

There's **bound** to be around £50 here – **sound** work, Shagpile!

I **might** have a **bright** idea. We could all go out for a **light** meal, if we can find the **right** place to eat.

We could see a film instead: **Flight Fright** is on in town. Or we could sit **tight** at home and watch the big **fight** on TV.

Watch out for words that have the letters **'ound'** and **'ight'**:

wounding sl**ight**ly r**ound**ed del**ight**ful

YOU CAN DO IT!

2 Hot stuff

Common letter strings
'exc'
'ough'

In the end the gang vote for Deej's idea. They go to a posh Indian restaurant and order the 'Emperor's Feast'.

Everyone **exclaimed** how **exciting** it was to be in an **exclusive** eating place.

This curry is **excellent**, **except** for its **excessive** heat!

The bhajis are **exceedingly** hot too!

The naan bread is **exceptional**!

Cheesy Chad says ...

I hope we have **enough dough** to pay for it, **though**.

What's the problem? We've checked **through** the prices **roughly**.

Don't get mixed up with words that begin with exe, like exercise and execution ...

Try to spot words containing **'ough'** & **'exc'**:

c**ough**ing   thr**ough**out   **exc**uses   **exc**elled

3 Podged!

Unbelievably, they manage to eat everything!

Common letter strings:
'eight'
'our'

My **weight** must be **eighty** kilograms now!

I scoffed **eighteen** poppadoms!

Ulf ate his own **height** in rice!

A waiter then asked them if they would like a one-**hour tour** of the kitchens.

You can see how we **pour** the sweet and **sour** sauce. **Your tour** will start in **four** minutes.

Joke Break

Phil: Why did you just eat that £2 coin?

Bill: It was my dinner money.

Here are some more '**eight**' and '**our**' words:
fr**eight**   overw**eight**   h**our**ly   f**our**teen

(4) Indoor shrews!

Three of the gang go on the tour of the restaurant kitchen.

Common letter strings:
'ould'
'shr'

I **would** like to be a chef if I **could**.

I **would**n't eat anything you made, Ulf – it **would** be m**ould**y!

You **should**n't have said that – you **should** apologise.

Just then, the kids heard a **shrill shriek** …

There's a **shrew** in that **shr**edded cabbage!

The kids **shrank** back, but the waiter just **shrugged**.

Light breakfast

Can you spell these '**ould**' and '**shr**' words?
couldn't   **would**'ve   **shr**ivelled   **shr**ewd

5 Ready, steady, crock!

Things start to go crazy in the kitchen.

Common letter strings:
'tch'
'ought'

The kids watched the chef **snatch** a cup and try to **catch** the shrew.

> He's no **match** for that top-**notch** rodent.

The chef slipped on a **patch** of oil and asked the kids to **fetch** him some **crutches**. Then the waiter **brought** the gang some news.

> I'm very sorry the chef **fought** that shrew during your tour. Because of this, I **thought** that we should charge you **nought** pounds for this meal.

Multiple Joyce

Which of these words is not spelt correctly?

A scratch
B hutch
C wretched
D zqhwhmxly

Watch out for other '**tch**' and '**ought**' words:

i**tch**y   pi**tch**ed   **ought**   s**ought**

Adding ing
A Day at the Movies

1 The excitement is growing

The Odd Mob are going on a day trip to the Moving Pictures film studios to see how movies are made.

The Odd Mob are looking forward to see**ing** and hear**ing** how movies are made. They hope they'll be meet**ing** lots of stars as they go walk**ing** around the sets. Deej has told Ulf he already looks like a famous movie star – Godzilla!

 When you add '**ing**' to most words the spelling of the word itself doesn't change:

do + ing = **do**ing   drink + ing = **drink**ing
eat + ing = **eat**ing

(2) Wozza learns her lessons

The Odd Mob arrive outside the Moving Pictures film studios. Wozza can't wait to buy a souvenir T-shirt.

Adding 'ing':
Words ending with a silent 'e'

Wozza's T-shirt should say 'I ❤ mov**ing** pictures', not 'I ❤ moveing pictures'.

Googal explains why and Wozza learns two things:

1. When you add 'ing' to a word that ends in a silent 'e' you drop the 'e'.
2. Never buy a cheap T-shirt from Mr Sumo.

Joke Break

Q. What did they get when they crossed a cocker spaniel, a poodle and a rooster for a new monster movie?

A: A Cockerpoodledoo!

When you want to add '**ing**' to words that end with a silent 'e', drop the 'e' and then add '**ing**':

bit**e** ▶ bit**ing**   hav**e** ▶ hav**ing**   writ**e** ▶ writ**ing**

YOU CAN DO IT!

③ An action hero

Flash is all action.

Adding 'ing': Words ending in 'ie'

Flash is on the set of an action movie. It's a nail-biting film where the villain tells **lie**s and the hero will **die** if someone doesn't **untie** him before the bomb the bad guy's left under his chair explodes.

Joke Break

Q. Why are movie stars so cool?

A: Because they've got loads of fans!

Flash dashes to the hero's rescue. She yells at the cops that the villain's **lying**. Then she gets busy **untying** the hero and saves him from **dying** just in the nick of time! But the director's cross. Flash isn't supposed to be in the movie – she's just supposed to watch it!

When a word ends in '**ie**' change the '**ie**' to '**y**' before adding '**ing**':

die ▸ d**ying**   lie ▸ l**ying**   tie ▸ t**ying**

4 Skippy the kangaroo

The director is hopping mad!

Adding 'ing': Double the consonant

Max and Googal are watching a film called 'Ho**pp**ing Sho**pp**ing' sta**rr**ing a kangaroo who's pla**nn**ing to go ski**pp**ing to the shops.

Max and Googal keep cla**pp**ing its every move. This means that the kangaroo keeps sto**pp**ing and hu**gg**ing them instead of playing its part.

The director is cha**tt**ing to a security guard but he's definitely not asking him to get Max and Googal's autographs ...

Cheesy Chad says ...

Remember, the **vowels** are the letters a, e, i, o and u. All the other letters in the alphabet are **consonants**.

Usually, if a word ends with a single vowel followed by a consonant, you **double the consonant** before adding '**ing**':

dr**op** ▸ dro**pp**ing   b**eg** ▸ be**gg**ing   d**ig** ▸ di**gg**ing

(But watch out for lim**it** ▸ limi**t**ing)

⑤ Up, up and away!

There's something in the air.

Adding 'ing':
Keep the
'y'

Is it a bird?
Is it a plane?

No – it's
SuperUlf!

Ulf's t**rying** to find the set of the
Superman film when a crane catches its
hook in his belt and whisks him up into
the air. Ulf's always wanted to be able to
fly like Superman – but this wasn't the
kind of fl**ying** he had in mind!

Joke Break

Q. What do you call an
overweight Superman?

A: Supperman.

When adding '**ing**' to all words ending in a consonant and
a '**y**', keep the '**y**':

s**py** ▸ s**py**ing   tr**y** ▸ tr**y**ing   fl**y** ▸ fl**y**ing

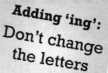

6 Shagpile Come Home

Shagpile fancies herself as a movie star.

Adding 'ing':
Don't change
the letters

The film company is looking for a dog to star in its latest movie: The Hound of the Basketballs. Shagpile doesn't want it to seem like she's cro**wing** about her acting ability but she thinks she's just right for the part.

The director's ca**lling**, 'Action!' The cameras are ro**lling** and Shagpile starts sh**owing** off by t**oing** and fr**oing** across the set with a basketball in her mouth. But she's so excited, she bites too hard and bursts the ball. With the director's words, 'You're fired!' echo**ing** in her ears, Shagpile legs it!

Multiple Joyce

Which of these words has an added 'ing'?

A Ding
B Dong
C Ping
D Ponging

When adding **'ing'**, to words ending in a **double letter** or an **'a'**, **'o'** or **'w'**, don't change those letters:

call ▶ ca**lling**   echo ▶ echo**ing**   row ▶ row**ing**

YOU CAN DO IT!

Words with Apostrophes

Something's missing

99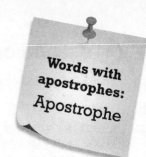

Words with apostrophes:
Apostrophe

1 It's an ill wind

Ulf is feeling under the weather.

Ulf thinks he is ill but Googal tells him he is fine –
he is just missing an apostrophe. This surprises
the rest of the Odd Mob as they thought he was
just missing a brain! Don't be like Ulf and spell
'I'll' as 'ill' – the **apostrophe** makes all the
difference.

apostrophe

When spelling, don't muddle up **words with
apostrophes** with words that sound like them:
'**We'll**' is not a wheel or a well.

② A ticklish situation

Deej makes sure Mr Sumo is up to scratch.

Words with apostrophes: Missing letters

Deej has put itching powder inside Mr Sumo's wrestling shorts. Mr Sumo told Deej's Mum and now Deej has got to write out five times:

I must not use itching powder on Mr Sumo.

He thinks this will take him ages, but Flash knows a quick way to spell '**must not**'. She tells him he can shorten '**I must not**' to '**I mustn't**' by **missing** out the '**o**' and using **an apostrophe** instead.

Apostrophes show that some **letters** are **missing** from a word:

do no**t** ▶ don**'t**   let **us** ▶ let**'s**   it **is** ▶ it**'s**

③ Don't ever change

Some things never change.

Words with apostrophes:
The first word stays the same

Where's that terrible pong coming from?

Mr Sumo's socks!

Cheesy Chad says ...

The first word in an apostrophe word almost never changes, e.g. **did** not = **did**n't.

Mind you, the Odd Mob think that Mr Sumo is a bit like an apostrophe word – they say he never changes his socks!

Watch out! 'Will not' is unusual. It shortens to 'won't'. You won't forget that, will you?

When spelling a new apostrophe word from two words, the **first word usually stays the same**:

would not ▶ **would**n't   **it** will ▶ **it**'ll

4) It's history

Max needs Googal's help.

I don't know what happens with the missing letters.

I think the postmen have to find them.

Max is confused. She knows that apostrophes go in place of missing letters so she's spelled '**shall not**' as '**sha'n't**' because she's left out both '**l**'s and the '**o**'.

But it's wrong. Max doesn't get it.

Googal explains that 'shall not' used to be spelled 'sha'n't' in the olden days but nowadays we **only use one apostrophe** when spelling a word with missing letters so it's spelled 'shan't'.

Be up-to-date: only use one apostrophe. I shan't say this again.

Joke Break

Q. What do you call a crocodile in a suit?

A: A snappy dresser.

When spelling a word with missing letters **only use one apostrophe**:

shan't   he'll   she'll   they'll

(5) The apostrophe game

Googal's made up a game for the Odd Mob.

> Words with apostrophes:
> Two words become one

Googal's game has one list of words with apostrophes and one list of words that don't have the letters missed out. The first person to match all the words together is the winner.

Words with apostrophes

Where's
She'll
We'd
Didn't
They'd
Could've

Words without apostrophes

We had
Did not
Where is
They had
Could have
She will

Everyone did well except Ulf – Shagpile ate his list. But Ulf said it was Googal's fault for using bone-flavoured paper.

Googal's answer sheet.

Where's   where is
She'll   she will
We'd   we had
Didn't   did not
They'd   they had

Multiple Joyce

Which of these is a shortened word?

A It's
B Tiny
C Little
D Weeny

Don't forget when you use an apostrophe to shorten a word you are making **one word** from two:

have not ▸ haven't   could not ▸ couldn't

Building Words
A Total Wash Out

1 Sock it to me

The gang have just returned from visiting Laundry World theme park. Surprisingly, it was a big disappointment.

> That rollercoaster was rubbish – I've never been on one pulled by a donkey.

> Yeah – no corkscrews, no drops, no loops and a 5 mph speed limit. Why was it called 'Obliteration'?

> I'm writing to complain about it, but how do you spell 'rollercoaster'.

Flash wrote down 'roll' and added 'er'. Then she wrote down 'coast' and added 'er' to that, to build the word 'rollercoaster' and spell it correctly.

> You can build it from words you know, Flash: start with 'roll' and 'coast'.

You can sometimes 'build' unknown spellings from words you know:

Knowing **edit** can help to spell **edit**ion.

YOU CAN DO IT!

② Dodgy dodgems

The Odd Mob discuss their disastrous day at Laundry World.

> I went on the ghost train – it was about as white knuckle as sunbathing.

> Shagpile and I tried Sockland. The '2,000 Years of Pantyhose' exhibition was a stinker!

Building words: Using root words

> I'm writing to complain about the dodgems. They were just old washing baskets on wheels. Goog, how do you spell 'dodgems'?

> It's another word you can build, Max – think about the word 'dodge'.

Cheesy Chad says ...

> There's a whole cracking section on root words on pages 8–12 of this book!

Max wrote dodge and added 'm' to make dodgem.

 'Dodge' is a **root word** that can help to spell other words:

dodger   dodgy   dodging   dodged

(3) Dodgy dodgems

Oh dear – the Odd Mob are still in a lather about their day out at the world's dreariest theme park.

Building words: Look for combined parts

> At least The Stain Removal Café was interesting – the tables were ironing boards.

> Well, one of the animatronic mops went wrong and attacked me so I'm complaining.

> A shame the burgers tasted of soap.

> At least you're clean! But don't tell me – you can't spell 'animatronic'?

Deej thought that *animatronic* might be a combination of 'animation' and 'electronic'. He was right!

Joke Break

Al: Have you seen the price of that hand wash?

Sal: No, I never watch soaps.

Build difficult new words from the parts that form them:
camcorder = **cam**era + re**corder**

④ Blacker than black

Some of the attractions at Laundry World were, well, unusual.

Building words: Building long words

Dye hard

Use words and endings that you recognise when building long words.

Some long words can be built up part by part:
sent ▶ present ▶ represent ▶ representation

⑤ Bleach holiday

But hang on, there were actually a couple of good things to recall about the day.

Building words:
More building words

Hey, remember when Ulf went in the giant tumble drier?

And when I won a tonne of fabric conditioner for pegging out 2 miles of washing in 10 minutes?

No, the best bit was when Mr Sumo fell out of the detergent log flume and shrank.

Yes, and he had to be accompanied by an adult for the rest of the day, tee hee ...

Multiple Joyce

Which of these can be built from the word 'fair'?

A flare
B unfair
C funfayre
D casserole

In fact, they're all going again next week!

Can you see ways to build these three tricky words:

conditioner (condition + er)

detergent (root word 'determined' or 'deterrent')

accompanied (root word 'company')

Dictionaries
Googal to the Rescue

> **Dictionaries:** Give the meaning of words

1 What does it all mean?

Is that a haiku sneaking up on the Odd Mob?

Joke Break

Gav: What's the definition of a teacher?

Bav: Someone who talks in my sleep.

The Odd Mob are arguing. Their teacher has told them to find out about haikus for their homework.

> They're tropical fighting fish.

> No they're not, they're pigeons with a really squeaky voice.

> Let's go to a pet shop and find out.

> You don't need a pet shop – you just need a dictionary.

Googal's right. A haiku is a poem, not a fish or a bird. So if you want to find out the **definition of a word** – look it up in the dictionary.

Cheesy Chad says ...

Sometimes words have more than one meaning. For example, the word 'crow' can mean a large black bird or boastful talking. So take care to choose the right definition.

A dictionary helps you **find the meaning of words**:

Dictionary – a book that gives the pronunciation and meaning of words.

(2) From aardvarks to zoology

It's as easy as ABC.

Dictionaries:
Alphabetical order

Ulf wants to know why 'aardvark' comes before 'ant' in the dictionary.

Why does aardvark come before ant in the dictionary?

It's because dictionaries list words in **alphabetical order**.

What's alphabetical order?

It's **ABC** order. A word beginning with the letter 'a' always comes before a word beginning with the letter 'b', and so on.

But ant and aardvark start with the same letter.

No problem! You look at the second letter in each word to see which one comes first. **A**ardvark is before **a**nt because 'a' comes before 'n' in alphabetical order.

Cheesy Chad says ...

If the first two letters in two words are the same, look at the third letter to put them in alphabetical order: cake, cap, cat

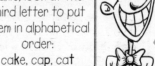

 Alphabetical order is when words are arranged in the same order as the letters of the alphabet:

ape **b**ear **c**at **d**og **e**lephant **f**rog **g**iraffe

YOU CAN DO IT!

③ I put a spell on you

Googal works some magic on Max's spelling.

Dictionaries:
Help you check spellings

> It's not Halloween, so why are you dressed up as a witch?

> I'm trying to spell words.

Max wishes she had a magic spell to help her spell. Googal tells Max the best way to sort out her spellings is to use a dictionary to look up words she's not sure how to spell. Then she can check that she's written them correctly.

Max gives it a go and before she can say 'abracadabra' her spelling improves.

Max's Diary

Beefour I usd a dikshunree to cek wuds mi speling wuz lik this.

But now I use a dictionary to check words my spelling is like this.

Joke Break

Nurse: Why did the chicken cross the playground?

Doctor: To get to the other slide.

A dictionary **helps** you **check spellings**:

bigin ✗	choclate ✗	gard ✗
begin ✓	chocolate ✓	guard ✓

④ It's not what you say it's the way that you say it

Googal wants the Odd Mob to pronounce words properly (prop-er-lee not prop-lee).

> Flash is an ath-a-leet.

> No, she's an ath-leet.

> I thought I was a runner.

Googal has been reading her dictionary and she's found out that the Odd Mob have been mispronouncing some words. For example, mischievous Deej is mis-che-vus not mis-chee-vee-us. And ticklish Wozza is tik-lish not tik-ill-ish. Mind you, Mr Sumo is still disastrous however you say it! (For the record, it's diz-as-trus not di-zas-ter-us.)

Cheesy Chad says ...

> Remember, the proper way to say pronunciation is 'pro-nun-see-A-shun' NOT 'pro-noun-see-A-shun'!

How to say the word

Probably
(prob-a-blee)

Dictionaries show you **how to pronounce** (say) **words** correctly:

library = li–bra-ree NOT li-bree
picture = pick-tcher, NOT pit-cher

⑤ A guiding word

See the sights with Shagpile.

Guide words show the first and last words on a page of a dictionary. They save time by helping you find the word you are looking for. For example, if the **guide words** on a page are *daft* and *dog* and the word you want is *Shagpile*, then don't waste time looking for it on that page because, alphabetically (and in real life), *Shagpile* doesn't come between *daft* and *dog*.

Guide Words

glade - glamour

glade an open space in a wood or forest

gladiator a man trained to fight at ancient Roman shows

glamour physical attractiveness

glance - glaze

glance quickly look

gland an organ in an animal

glare look fiercely

glass a hard surface

glaze fit with glass

Guide words are found at the top of each page in the dictionary. On the page with the **guide words** *smash – smug* you will find the words:

smell   smile   smooth

Because, alphabetically, **sme**, **smi** and **smo** come after **sma** but before **smu**.

6 Herbivores and verbivores

Ulf needs help.

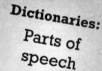

Dictionaries: Parts of speech

> If herbivores eat herbs, do verbivores eat words?

> Only if they're absolutely starving.

Ulf is fed up. For homework he's got to sort a list of words into nouns, pronouns, verbs, adverbs and adjectives. The problem is that Ulf wouldn't know a noun, pronoun, verb, adverb or adjective even if they bit him on the bottom!

Googal tells him that if he looks the words up in the dictionary, the dictionary will tell him what **part of speech** they are, e.g. a noun, pronoun, verb, adverb, adjective, preposition or conjunction.

Multiple Joyce

Which of these words won't you find in a dictionary?

A Apple
B Ball
C Cat
D Dzzzxxng

A dictionary will tell you what **part of speech** the word is that you're looking up. Sometimes words can be used in more than one way:

joke: **(noun)** *Thing said or done to cause laughter; amusing or ridiculous thing.*

(verb) *To make jokes; talk in a humourous way.*

Spell Checkers
Word You Believe It?

> **Spell checkers:**
> Can spot spelling mistakes

1 The present tense

It's just after Christmas and the Odd Mob are writing thank-you letters for the presents they were given. As usual, Googal is checking what they've written.

The spelling here is shocking! According to these letters, we've been given a 'Sympsons DVD', an 'Adedaz hudi', a 'bower konstricta', a 'batree mullteepac', a 'Britknee Spiers CD' and a 'sqoch raccit'.

We'd better do the letters on a computer and use a spell checker then.

 Computer **spell checkers** can help you to spot spelling mistakes.

2 Battered and bare

Deej re-writes his letter on a computer.

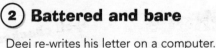

Dear Auntie Soshal,
Thank you so much for my
64 batree mullteepac. I will
now have enough batrees
to keep my MP3 player
going until Monday.
Love from Deej.

The squiggly lines mean that the software thinks that Deej may have spelt these three words wrong. He right clicks 'batree' to see the computer's suggestions for the correct spelling:

bay tree
bare
battery
battered

Hey, look at all the cool ways to spell battery!

Cheesy Chad says ...

Watch out because spell checkers may suggest American spellings sometimes too, such as color, traveling, defense. Make sure that your software is set to 'UK English'.

 Most computer **spell checkers** will help you to correct spellings by making suggestions. Only one is right!

YOU CAN DO IT!

(3) Grey boots for Max

Max is next to type up her thank-you letter on the computer. Her first effort had lots of mistakes ...

> Hi there Great-great grandad,
> The <u>Sympsons</u> DVD you <u>bort</u> for me is <u>grayt</u>.
> Ta very <u>mutch</u>,
> Max

Spell checkers: Can make wrong suggestions

Next, Max tried some of the suggestions made by the spell checker.

> Hi there Great-great grandad,
> The Symptoms DVD you boot for me is grey.
> Ta very munch,
> Max

There, that's far better.

Oh dear; somehow I don't think she chose the right suggestions ...

Mr Sumo was having a lot of problems with his new PC.

With **spell checkers**, take care when deciding which suggestion is the correct word.

(4) A terrible racket

Flash was very pleased with the letter she typed on the computer.

> Dear cousin Dash,
> I am sow pleased with the grate squash racket yew got four me. Everyone hear nose eye play sports awl the thyme.
> Buy from Flash.

Look – there's not a single squiggly line. I made no spelling mistakes at all!

You nutter! Ten of your words are the wrong ones – they just happen to be correct spellings of completely different words.

Cheesy Chad says ...

This is often a problem with homophones – words that sound the same but have different meanings.

Be careful! Computer **spell checkers** won't spot mistakes where the error is a real word with a different meaning:

I brushed my hare.

⑤ My kinda music

Finally, HMD tries typing his letter.

Spell checkers: Beware of places and names

Hey Granny dude,
It was kind of you to send me that Britney Spears CD all the way from Eggyham. I will put it in my collection, alongside my Megadoom, Thrashpox and Dedder Than Dedd albums.
Yours heavily, HMD

Hey, this machine's useless, man. It says all those band names are spelt wrong but I copied them off the official websites. Eggyham is right too.

They are correct, HMD – it's just that computer spell checkers don't recognise all places and names. Now, where's the dicshunry I got for Kristmus?

Multiple Joyce

Which of these has been 'corrected' by a spell checker?

A Ant & Deck
B Antandec
C Ant & Dec
D Beetle and Doc

Some **spell checkers** cannot correct places and names, so **check them yourself!**

Adding 'ed'
Liar, Liar, Pants on Fire

(1) Let sleeping dogs lie

Deej is boasting about his 2-million track music
collection; Flash says she's faster than a meteorite;
HMD claims he is the world's best guitarist and Ulf says
he can eat concrete. Googal is fed up.

Googal is worri**ed**. Has HMD fibb**ed**? Are you confus**ed**?
Notice how all these **verbs** end in '**ed**'.

> '**ed**' is a common verb ending that shows the **past tense**:
> lie ▸ lied   boast ▸ boasted   worry ▸ worried

137

(2) No butts

It turned out to be true! HMD, Deej, Flash and Ulf really have entered the UK Lying Championships. They continue to practise.

Adding 'ed': Verbs ending in 'e'

Bottom drawer

Look how the verbs **pose** and **race** are changed to **posed** and **raced**.

For **verbs** ending in '**e**', just add a '**d**' to form the past tense:

dare ▶ dared   like ▶ liked   provide ▶ provided

3) Ha ha bonk

The lying continues!

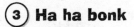

Adding 'ed':
Verbs ending in two consonants

Wayne Rooney rang to **ask** me to help him with free kicks.

So what? Lionel Messi **asked** me to be his personal trainer. So did Jessica Ennis and Roger Federer.

When I tell a joke, people **laugh** for three hours.

Big deal. I told a joke yesterday and a man **laughed** his head off, then his arms and legs off too.

Cheesy Chad says ...

Remember, consonants are all the letters of the alphabet except for the vowels a, e, i, o, u.

Notice how the verbs **ask** and **laugh** are changed to **asked** and **laughed** by adding '**ed**'.

Just add '**ed**' to verbs ending in **two consonants**:

start ▶ started   roll ▶ rolled   wish ▶ wished

④ Blow up your candles, dear

Who is telling the best lies? It's hard to decide.

Adding 'ed': Verbs ending in one vowel and a consonant

*I can **rip** a phone directory in half with my hands.*

*Feeble! When I was a toddler I **ripped** a sofa in half with my elbows.*

*My mum made me a 5-metre birthday cake and decided to **top** it with solid gold candles.*

*Pfff! My mum **topped** my 20-metre cake with diamonds and dynamite. The party went off with a bang!*

The verbs **rip** and **top** above need a **double consonant** when 'ed' is added.

For words ending with **one vowel and a consonant**, double the consonant when '**ed**' is added:

hum ▸ hu**mm**ed   beg ▸ be**gg**ed   fit ▸ fi**tt**ed

⑤ Heading for the sun

The lying was getting worse ...

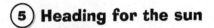

Adding 'ed':
Verbs ending in two vowels and a consonant

I've been told I **look** like a film star.

Yeah – I was told you **looked** like Shrek.

I fancy a holiday next week – I might **head** for Saturn.

I **headed** for the sun last week, in a rocket - hence my lovely tan.

Joke Break

Jim: Are you going to Saturn on Friday?

Kim: Yep – when I get back I'll give you a ring.

The verbs **look** and **head** have a **double vowel** which means that the final consonant is **not** doubled when 'ed' is added.

For verbs ending with **vowel**, **vowel**, **consonant**, just add '**ed**':

fail ▸ failed   seem ▸ seemed   cool ▸ cooled

6 A late lie in

It's the next day and the lies have finally stopped (thank goodness).

Adding 'ed': Words ending in consonant plus 'y'

HMD, when did you **apply** to enter the Lying Championships? Has there been a **reply**?

Erm, I **applied** last week. They **replied** to say we missed the closing date – and, sadly, that's not a lie.

That's a shame – Googal said we would have won for sure.

Really?

You're not the only ones to tell fibs, tee hee!

Notice how the word **apply** changes to **applied** in the past tense, and **reply** to **replied**.

For verbs ending in **consonant + y**, change the 'y' to 'i' and add **'ed'**:

try ▸ tried   cry ▸ cried   supply ▸ supplied

7 An exceptional report

Ulf decided to go to the UK Lying Championships anyway. He comes back very excited.

> I weared my best clothes and I runned all the way there. I sitted next to a girl who sayed she heared that we putted in our entry late. I'm sure we would have beated the other teams and winned the cup.

Oh dear, Ulf has forgotten that there are **exceptions** to the rules about adding '**ed**' to verbs. Googal helped him out with a list:

To make the past tense:

wear ▸ wore (not 'weared')
run ▸ ran (not 'runned')
sit ▸ sat (not 'sitted')
say ▸ said (not 'sayed')
hear ▸ heard (not 'heared')
put ▸ put (not 'putted')
beat ▸ beat (not 'beated')
win ▸ won (not 'winned')

Multiple Joyce

Which of these is correct?

A Knowed
B Knewed
C Knew
D Kold

And that's the truth!

Index